Biographies of Runaway Dogs

Troy Schoultz

Biographies of Runaway Dogs ©2016 by Troy Schoultz. Published in the United States by Vegetarian Alcoholic Press. No part of this work may be reproduced in any form without the author's consent. For information, contact vegalpress@gmail.com

Some of these poems first appeared in the following publications: *Cooweescoowee, Chiron Review, Free Verse, The Kerf, Midwestern Gothic, Misfit Magazine, The Muse, Nerve Cowboy, SEEMS, Scars TV.*

Cover art: *Love Shack* by Julia Flanagan

Cover design and photography by Amie Brownfield

The Biographies of Runaway Dogs   9

Empty Farmhouses   11

Expect Rain   13

Best Wishes, Janet Gaynor   15

Forget About the Sound of Her Voice
When It's 3 a.m. and Snowing   17

For The Girls Whose Names Once Graced
Toilet Stalls   18

Tackling Shoplifters   19

Faith Apts.   21

Even The Cemeteries Were Once Brand New
For Don Winter   23

No Reasonable Offer Refused   24

Miss Andrissi's Vodka Bottles   26

Downings Bar   28

Adams County, WI, Summer 1994	30
The Suicide of Someone I Should Remember	32
Women Dreaming of Deer	34
1988	37
Forgetting Names	39
Beyond (Murdock & Harrison Street)	41
Lake Petenwell, Mid-1970's	43
Single	45
What My Father Talks About While Drinking Beer	46
Lucid Dreams of Former Residence	48
July 1982	50

Eulogy For A Landlord
For Louie Borden   51

Seer of Angels and Demons   53

For Doug Flaherty

This being a book primarily of memories both real and imagined, I would also like to thank all the teachers in and out of classrooms and with or without degrees who have entered my life and blessed me with invaluable wisdom, headaches, and experience. This is also for all the runaway dogs, past and present, as well as those who've decided to stay.

"The truth is overrated."

- Paul Westerberg

The Biographies of Runaway Dogs

These humid July afternoons are meant
for remembering women who may have well long
forgotten you
and minor miracles you were an unfit witness for.
It's too early to go out and too late
to plan anything that might salvage the day.

You think about a story
your once possible wife told you, a childhood memory
about a neighborhood dog, neglected,
who made a run for freedom after well over a year
of straining against the chain, so driven that the spike
screwed into Wisconsin clay dirt
in a kennel left open was ripped from the earth.
And so he ran, directionless but hard,
a life behind chain links, ask yourself,
what would you do? Across the burnt grass yard
through the ditch and onto the highway, blossoming
with raw joy, almost across when the trailing chain
hooked a passing truck. His neck snapped, a violent
somersault, dragged a few yards, killed.

You consider that dog and the woman who could've
been your wife and raise a toast to them in your mind.
Afternoons like this you still wish
you were out of your mind,
still able to afford all you believed you could lose.

Empty Farmhouses

You see them off highways marked
with carcasses of dead deer, eyes still open
tongues out, bemused by minuscule length
of their disposable meat lives.
Scattered wrecked holdouts along the back roads
that used to be the highways. Gutted,
flaking lead paint, buckled roof and doorways
with cataract windows. The thin scar of gravel
through tall grass like a fossilized snake
marks the ghost of a driveway.
I eye them on my drive home from
whatever crises I have lived each day.
I want to take the first exit, find my way
to the forgotten highway, follow that
scar of gravel as far as the snake allows,
wade through the cut grass and paintbrush,
survey the stone foundations fashioned by
hands now bone and dust,
step across the threshold like a widower groom,
breathe in the decay and old memories
like a wine snob in a goblet.
bask in the gutted solitude, weave your way
through rooms asunder, pick up broken dishes,
found objects waiting for human touch
once again. Take a seat on an unbroken chair
and watch the autumn sunset through a shattered pane,
listen to something crawl and chew within the walls,

tell yourself
only the insane
choose to not be hermits.

Expect Rain

You can expect the couch

that fit through the door

with exact precision

to have somehow expanded.

Expect rain on the day

of borrowed open air trailers.

You never leave spaces

completely absent of the residue

of a life lived: abandoned lamps

with shades tilted a rakish angle,

theme park coffee cups, that shot glass

unused in the cupboard

untouched and left for the next,

that rotary phone you found in the attic

waiting on long-distance calls

from Edison's ghosts.

Try as you might to be prepared,

months ahead of time

you will scrub and scrap and haul

until you feel your heart eat itself mid-pulse

if you don't find a way of getting out before

nightfall. Expect the security deposit

to never find its way to your new mailbox.

You find yourself at an age

where it seems too late

to be a nomad in exit,

moving in together

and all too often

moving out alone.

Best Wishes, Janet Gaynor

Old-timer Lyle visits me
at work on rainy Sunday afternoons,
bringing postcards, sports cards,
newspaper clippings,
spilling nicotine-tainted artifacts
into the guard station.

His auction sale conquests are bound
scrapbooks, wide as coffee tables,
bought on sight,
regardless of contents.
Most lithographs of windmills
and children, depression-era Halloweens,
magazine ads from the 1950's and '60's,
movie magazine icon photos
with autographs and captions:
Carol Lombard, Clark Gable, Shirley Temple,
Janet Gaynor offering up best wishes
from fading sheets of cardboard.

"I imagine she was an old woman," says Lyle shrugging,
his face a relief map of third shift survival,
"Maybe sometimes that's all they had, a bound book
of things they liked to sit and look at."

I imagine her as well,
house or even chair-bound,

her milky eyes taking in the joy
of soup and dish detergent without
distraction of text, daydreams of possessing
alabaster shoulders and pillar sexuality
of Lombard, wishing Clark Gable would
wink at her, awakening
her private Janet Gaynor in hibernation,
asking for a dance on a rotating platform
just like during the filming of *Gone With The Wind*
because Gable
couldn't dance to save his life.

Forget About the Sound of Her Voice When It's 3 a.m. and Snowing

Instead, concentrate on how
the house across the way
resembles a wistful rectangular skull,
windows given eyes of intellect
by way of electric holiday candles.
Imagine the blizzard as falling purity
reflecting streetlight, a glowing gift,
teaser of dawn. Enjoy the lack of headlights,
a police or ambulance siren
the sole whisper proof of the living.

Instead, brace yourself for these colorless months
and abbreviated days
relearning to sleep in the middle
of a queen size bed, dreaming
of lilacs, mosquitoes, and rain.

For The Girls Whose Names Once Graced Toilet Stalls

You walked between classes, your hair
veiling your face with eyes
cast down on swirling tiled floor.
You were the talk of morning study hall,
your name a magic marker headline
on vendetta tiles. Your shade of eye shadow
was your penalty, you held textbooks
against your breasts, a shield
against varsity team leers. "Slut."
That word flowed effortlessly
off adolescent tongues like shower water
down a locker room drain
until you yourself
believed it to be true.

May you have all made
your grand escape, wherever you are.
May you come to learn trust
streaming with the sun
through venetian blinds to awaken you,
your walk straight and defiant, your name
not scrawled in jagged lines but in calligraphy
by a hand smoother than summer, a hand
of one who lights the doorway,
waiting, saying, "I've missed you,"
before your shoes can leave your feet.

Tackling Shoplifters

Pushing shopping carts in the snow,
a thermos of schnapps hidden
from the managers in the parcel pick-up area,
it was thirty below, wind chill inclusion.
This is how
I celebrated the death of the 1980's,
working part-time, tackling shoplifters
no younger or poorer than I,
singing to myself in the backroom
feeling as lost as a chance
with a drunken dream girl
who had no chance
to find me again
once the cops closed the party down.
We drank together, all us 24-hour lost souls,
made mix tape soundtracks
of the hours and days we'd kill,
those promises spilling off beer-heavy tongues,
"You should move on college boy,
wasting your life in frozen food aisles..."
with box cutter knives, hoping the '90's
and our bad luck would finally
pay off in some dim way.
That night, a rented motel room,
a bathtub of ice and bottles,
captured and lost somewhere on video,
we held on to our lives at that point
like icicle-adorned handles of shopping carts

outside during the last day of December
or maybe the ankles of a panicked kid
falling face first on hard tile
broke and desperate for a pack of Marlboro Lights.

Faith Apartments

There's a man outside the local Pick'n'Save

who plays a forgotten waltz on his accordion among

racked shopping carts every Tuesday evening at sundown.

People walk past him as if he's a ghost. He believes in his art

and will not betray it.

My downstairs neighbor drives with a statue of Buddha

in the passenger seat. My grandparents

had their plastic, painted saints

anchored in the pinholes of the dashboard speakers,

conspiring in the Polish tongue

with me in the backseat, convinced an act of faith

alone could deflect safety glass.

We all ride with our chosen gods.

An old man lives in the gothic church across the street.

It was renovated into apartments, looks haunted,

even the noonday sun in late July, all eyes

cataract with damaged blinds and box fans.

The man sits out front on the curb in the summer,

the belfry casting foreshadows upon him.

Shirtless, he watches the cars pass, dreaming

of time travel, imagines the age

of V-8 engines, tin beer cans, bullet bras, and filter-less smokes.

He blares the era of Eisenhower from a black, battered boombox.

Martini lullabies of Frankie, Dino, The Platters, and Rosemary Clooney

spill out on to Isabella St. and rise with the post-rain steam

from the asphalt like phantoms after the rain dares

to fall like a hammer from late July sun.

Even The Cemeteries Were Once Brand New
For Don Winter

I'm no longer young, but somehow
I've managed to dodge real tragedy.
This much is bearable: the promise of passings,
daily troubles consistent as rain.
Still tomorrow's injuries are flashing blades
like back alley thieves. It's the minutiae
of trials that will make you lose your mind
if you dwell on them too long,
a lifetime of paper cuts, unexpected bills,
blown transmissions and emergency room runs.
Simple miracles lying before us
like wrapped packages are what are meant to save us,
disposable moments of lightning ecstasy that make us
clutch on to life like a lover at an airport.
Someone once told me, "It seems bad enough now,
but wait another year. This won't matter anymore
and you'll have a whole new set troubles to worry
about."
We lose ourselves wishing on dead stars still shining,
laughing into the black drawer of midnight
the ferocious beauty of all that is temporary.

No Reasonable Offer Refused

When she offers you a seat on the couch,
do not assume familiarity, do not be surprised
when she takes her seat on the ottoman facing you.

It's been a few years since your initial parting
but she still has that bowl, the one your grandmother
gave you, glass the shape and color
of fallen leaves in autumn. For a split second,
you think this all to be a mistake.
Better to have left your porch unlocked,
let her drop it off when you weren't home.

You sip your iced tea slowly. You don't want to leave
but realize you don't quite belong.

She is moving across country, taking only what will fit
in her car. "It's just stuff," she says,
"and there will always be more." You think maybe
this is wisdom you could use.
You eye up a stack of LPs in the corner,
talk her into letting you buy a live Rolling Stones
and Todd Rundgren disc for a dollar each.

Shadows take up the bare apartment walls. The talk has
come to a stalemate. You stand up and motion her
toward you,
hug her, tell her you'll never see her ever again.

She doesn't argue. Take the last of yourself from her home,
her life. Now walk out into the sun. Begin again.

Miss Andrissi's Vodka Bottles

Miss Andrissi favored pants over dresses and men's
dress shirts
over blouses, dark hair pulled murky and sullen behind
her head.
The most enthusiasm she could muster was
a dark, cynical bemusement, no blame. It couldn't
have been comfortable being an atheist and a fan of The
Pretenders teaching
at a Catholic grade school in 1981.
The only thing she probably had in common with her
colleagues
was hidden bottles. In the dragging months leading to
graduation,
too close to the summer before high school,
recess sports and kickball faded to our sullen roaming
of the school grounds of Sacred Heart.
While trying the locks of faculty cars, a familiar
cargo was exposed in the back of Miss Andrissi's
hatchback:
plastic bottles of IGA vodka, the same kind favored by
vagrants,
found empty in back lots and by the track,
a misplaced relic of degeneracy among the sanctified.
Only
two out of three were emptied.
Kevin Fekete, two years away from death, might've
helped himself
to one of the full, hidden it in the shrubs only to be

retrieved under nightfall with the help of an older criminal brother
with car keys if not a license.

Fast forward, post-high school graduation, pre-disillusion,
pre-desperate for stability, current with no fucks left to give,
a hot July sundown, a buddy and I, for no goddamn good reason
whatsoever were parked in his uninsured tank of a '72 Oldsmobile
at Sacred Heart's faculty parking lot.
We were downing the better part of a twelve-pack of Old Style.
I don't know what it was that lead us to ending
up the day at the scene of previous crimes, but when the patrol car
turned the corner, we spilled out and scattered through backyards
and clotheslines, I toward my parent's home and he to
his future wife's apartment. Were we celebrating Miss Andrissi or
just bored and unemployed in Central Wisconsin
with an illegal 12-pack and gas to burn? Taking a short cut,
I ran through the foundry yard among dead machines that called out to me,
"Brass in Pocket" playing on loop through my young inebriated skull.

Downings Bar

Our old class president serves
Another pitcher of watery light beer
Same ass-kissing grin seven years worn thin
In the pages of high school yearbooks packed away
Any more surprises here
In red neon Budweiser glow
Where young mill workers sit and smoke
Alongside old married couples who forgot
How to talk to one another in a paper city Friday night
No generation gap
Between melting ice cubes
In bar rail mixer glasses
Blank slumped drained sapped
And not even drunk enough yet
I read each face like the local news
The rain-stained ceiling tiles above me
Tells an unread story
I wander in
Half in the bag
To the piss-perfumed men's room
Where a large greasy man
Spills his bladder into the dilapidated sink
And stumbles out into smoke and dim
I read the words of local sages
Scrawled in hatred carved in sorrow

In the dim pool table light a glass is shattered

And a sage poet recites his toilet stall serenade
To his crying woman
Her face is painted like sunset
And the night slips off into
Polluted murky
Factory
Rivers

Adams County, WI, Summer 1994

The punch clock on the grime-caked wall offered me
three hours until last call. I drove from the factory
streaked
and blackened with asphalt sealant
like the second shift undead to drink
cheap rail mixers and smoke Camel Lights
with the other breathing, bleeding ghosts
at roadside taverns. Some nights would find me
with a carry-out twelve-pack of Old Style
back at a co-worker's trailer home,
falling asleep under the box air conditioner
on a slip-covered sagging sofa. Other nights
I'd drive the backroads beyond the county line
through the haze of late summer night heat
mumbling a blood/alcohol prayer,
left hand on the wheel, the other
reaching for the backseat cooler. I'd drive
until a tinge of orange whisper crept up behind
the jack pine silhouette of forests spotted with
unmarked graves
of informants from Chicago brought up north in luxury
cars,
gun barrels against their temples, incoherent, pissing
themselves,
maybe calling out a final plea bargain
for God to save them from Hell's tired yawn.

I was younger then, and lost,

drinking, driving, waiting, believing
that nothing good could come from anything I did
under that heavy wolf moon that followed me
to sunrise and sleep. Those nights were graphite
greasing the machinery of my waking hours,
avoiding friction of pieces around me
susceptible to flame.

The Suicide of Someone I Should Remember

The first giveaway is the phrase "died at home
unexpectedly." The second is the autobiographical tone
of the obituary. Apparently, we worked at the same
supermarket
twenty or so years ago. All I'm offered are details
designed to ignite memories but I can't even recall
her face. This fact wears me down for the afternoon.
There are others who took a similar exit whom I do
recall.
I imagine what it might have been
that finalized the solitary negotiation.
perhaps they were dealt a curse of insight
we are blissfully unaware. I summon these thoughts
at the worst possible moments.

Serenity doesn't come easy when or even if it comes
at all. There is no swimming upstream, no trajectories,
without collision but there are instances of reprieve
like fireworks at midnight allowing the shadows
to loosen their grip on your throat. There are mites of
dust
in a ballet on a slice of sunlight, wood smoke from a
distant
fire in autumn, a beautiful woman singing, swaying and
silent
behind safety glass at a traffic light turned red.

Our worlds will end several times within our lives

but maybe if I hold on long enough to be an old man,
things of gold will come to me and you. We fix our eyes
on the fiery clouds at sunset as wolves lazily gather
in the fields outside the picture window. We pull the
blinds,
sing a song or two,
love each other as strongly as we are able,
waiting until morning.

Women Dreaming of Deer

She survived PTSD and keeps strange hours

watching TV shows about magicians

at 3a.m. and stays forever positive. She

tells me that she dreams often. I struggle

to hold on to mine before waking.

She tells me of a dream of a deer breaking into her house

without explanation of how. Hooves have difficulties

picking locks or wedging open windows.

I tell her that deer in dreams

signify femininity, gentleness, and grace. All the things

that keep the masculine on this side of disaster.

She questions the grace part, says she stumbles

through life too often.

A former girlfriend once told me

that she slept with a married man. She drove

to his place afterhours, his wife and children

states away. She admitted fascination with family

portraits on the walls. The sex

was rougher than she'd expected,

she admitted fear. In the morning,

as she fumbled for clothes and keys,

she spotted movement in the corner of her eye.

Gathered

at the patio door, a herd of does

wet black noses pressed against the glass.

My father fed corn to deer in a clearing, beating

the empty plastic pail like a shaman's drum

until they appeared like ancestral ghosts.

He once hunted, but lost the taste for the kill.

He brewed an appreciation for grace and elegance,

Claiming that on each birthday a doe he took a

particular

liking for would appear to present her new fawns.

Somewhere an elderly woman rustles under a heavy

quilt,

awakening to another autumn morning, a lucid dream of

drums

beyond the frost-tainted window and among the pines,

hooves scratching the forest floor, the distant percussion

of gunpowder, darting the bullet until the moon climbs

above branches.

1988

We stumbled, crawled, vomited
through Polaroid summers.

Diplomas were shoved
in our hands with a back-slap,
a fake grin, and a please don't
come back here ever again.

There was always a party
in someone's rented dive,
all beer-soaked shag carpet
and fist-punctured paneling.

I was usually the last to leave,
trying to gel decadence
and minimum wage,
hitting on drunk girls, the kind
that laugh too loud,
with skinny-dipper eyes.

I was naïve, juiced, pathetic,
playing a smooth Houdini of lock and chain hearts.

I strolled before dawn
across empty bottles and prone bodies
with someone's mix tape and pack of Camels
like a shining Buddha of alcohol and wrong turns.

I kicked the screen door open, stared
through the lead apron of night
with Li Po eyes, waiting on the epic.

Forgetting Names

It's painful enough
feeling grateful for some old-timer
calling you a "young man" at 40
but memory's betrayal is cruelty,
a click switch death mechanism,
a slow, erasing crawl.
You associate the faces
until they too start to dim.

That cashier, a girl with a strawberry birthmark
and sunlight hair, you snuck her home
late night after work
to drink up your father's beer.

The elderly tough-guy security guard
who offered advice, loved sweets,
wore a red tux and brought a hooker
as a date to his ex-wife's wedding,
swore that if there was a hell
then that was where he was headed.

That mustachioed portly guy
who adored bad '70's music
and got you sick on some drink
called Cement Mixers,

The too young to be married college student

who spent time homeless in Europe
living among skinheads,
who made you mix tapes you mourn losing
on those nights you need to listen.

They have all wandered through your rentals,
leaving layers of paint, tossing handfuls
of seed where weeds would overtake them,
carving pocket-knife initials
on your park bench life.

Beyond (Murdock & Harrison Street)

Our neighborhood died all around us
in building, blood, and bone. Across the way,
a chimney rose above factory rubble, giving
the finger to all the wrecking balls of the world,
a partial wall and furnace standing, bricks jagged as bad dentistry,
fall-out and failure christened in spray paint and shattered glass.

The elderly drunk next door rolled his own cigs,
raised tomatoes and cucumbers through sawed-off plastic
bottles of cheap brandy and vodka. Cinderblocks suspended
a crude flame-job hot-rod up the alley, a leaf-filled hot-tub surrounded
by crabgrass and dogshit beyond backyard shrubs.

Under streetlight I spoke with a man two houses down
as he kept his Jack Russel barely contained at the end of
a leash.
The next morning his heart broke free of a leash of its own.
Next of kin gathered for a yard sale, fire pit and half barrel
on the lawn, a lifetime of power tools, fishing tackle,
and folding tables.

You left a ring with a note attached under our steamed mirror.
So I found another house prone to gravity in another dying neighborhood
with rain-water basement lakes and squirrels shifting in the attic.
I drank homemade rail-mixers and watched the walls bloom
with fresh coats of paint, mastering the discipline of amnesia.

Some days there was sunlight left in my ribcage.
Most nights I simply longed to burn.

Lake Petenwell, Mid-1970's

A few campsites over, a local motorcycle club circled
the bonfire, fueled on cheap booze, drugs, fireworks.
Roman candles arched, plumed above the tents,
exploding lightning hue,
jarring the campground into false daylight.

My uncle was a number of years away
from the jungles of Vietnam.
Drunken explosions and outraged tears of tires and
gears
tore him back to war relics in my grandparents' attic.
A candle blast came too close to my one cousin's head.

We took cover in campers and tents. My uncle
grabbed a bat and walked toward an inferno
silhouetted by man and machines. One swing of the bat
separated a rider from his ride. My uncle
would've dragged him to the lake,

held him underwater, would've drowned him
if the county hadn't arrived.

I realized things ugly and dangerous exist
and have their way of seeping into anything
sacred as a summer night by a lake and campfire
when the only bright things arching across the sky

should be wishful things.

Single

All I'm trying to say
is that I don't miss the gleaning knives
that grew from our tongues.
I do still miss your arms after dark
but I traded our lives
for a one bedroom apartment,
no lease, paid water,
with appliances
and self-cleaning oven,

and tonight
I'm far gone on this brandy.

What I mean to tell you is
the moon panicked last night
and my heart raised hell
like a jailed drunk
who even after the beatings
refuses to go down.

What My Father Talks About While Drinking Beer

We crack the fresh pop-tops
from the garage refrigerator,
an avocado-colored refugee from the 1970's
still humming. He takes a good
long pull from his, a lager watery and weaker
than the darks and stouts I'm used to. He says light beer
helps him keep his edge. After two more sweat-beaded
cans he begins to open up. Talks about
the young nuns at his Catholic high school,
fantasizes about the sleek white swimsuits
underneath the layers of black and grey,
says he hates church, prefers the marsh
at sunset, swears he and a buddy saw Satan
in a a denim jacket and eyes like sparklers
drinking in a tavern at the Illinois border in 1972.
He tells of the teacher who chastised
him for watching ditch diggers
from the classroom window, how she told
him that was all he'd amount to.
He asked her what were they doing
that was wrong? Where was the crime
in irrigation? As I'm taken aback
by the dignity of that response,
he goes on to say that years later
when he found himself at the roadside
laying pipe, deep in soil, he wished
that same teacher would drive past.

He would raise his shovel in the July sun shouting in personal victory, "I've made it! I've finally made it!"

Lucid Dreams of Former Residence

I pass structures, spray-painted, condemned, fallen,
and they rise like the bored or damned
through rich pungent asphalt.

I walk their rooms again,

my mind stepping across worn carpet, stealing glances
at peeling plaster before slow-motion
diving through milky window panes,
all sunshine and Polaroid colors.

The ripe green blades
rush forth to kiss me.

There have been many empty nights spent
alone, emptier nights
spent with others, vagrant squirrels
squatting in the attic, dead voices asking,
"Why?" from the crawlspace, furnaces
wrenched loose and set to yawn a sweet little hell.

There has been wall punctuation
with fists and boots and rusty keys
into the wrong locks,
love full-blown and minimalized
shedding dogs, Sunday papers,
coffee cups and handcuffs,

lost jobs and God's little hand-outs,
engagement rings and diabetic cats,
lilacs and drunken phone calls,
garage beams, nylon rope, and Christmas wreaths,
cigarettes pushing against my forearms
through photos of her and beyond.

I reach, god-like through every room,
not ready to abandon this dingy past
from my waking life. A face I recognize
from every ragged window resembles mine,
a flood of dancing faces and eyes
washing thick and gelatin
down the streets and avenues
I held as high and lonesome as any place
I ever dared call my home.

July 1982

I helped Mark Edwards deliver the Daily Tribune
one afternoon the summer before we traded
Catholic grade school for a public high,
weaving through driveways and city blocks
riding bikes with banana seats, wearing t-shirts
with silly-assed sayings.

Mark knew who was working or on vacation,
which garages stored liquor.

We made our own fringe benefits
sitting on the softball bleachers
passing back and forth
a stolen half-pint of Southern Comfort,
the sun a flaming balloon, the grass
deeper than any Crayola hue,
the world a prematurely aged
and overripe Polaroid snapshot.

I rode unsteadily to Major's Drug Store
and bought an issue of *Mad* magazine
the cover proclaimed Pac-Man
Man of the Year.

Eulogy For A Landlord
For Louie Borden

His last advisory gems were:

1. Get yourself a "honey" to share
   the rent with, if nothing else.

2. You are one hell
   of a good-looking guy,
   but lose about 25-30 pounds.

3. Get a goddamn life.

He died on my birthday.
Few things more bracing
than house-bound men
hooked to oxygen telling you
to get a life.

But he was forgiven tenfold,
last of a kind,
choosing truth over plastic tact,
taking pulls and drags
off hand-rolled cigs and cases of Blatz,
dealing cribbage cards
until the sweetest end.

As a kid he loved comic books

and to steal free into movies.
He made WW2
sound like the time of his life,
a heavy-artillery frat party in France
with sweet women,
unworldly wine and nightly dances.
The plainest girl was always the one to pick.
She would cradle your war-gutted heart,
listen to your broken French,
love you with an instinctive power
pretty girls could never understand.

He gambled with friends,
birthed carnations and tomatoes toward heavy
bloom,
ventured out for drinks at The Cheating Heart.
I was glad to see him in a flannel shirt,
sans make-up in his casket
garnished at the wake
with tobacco pouches,
packs of playing cards,
and 3 Musketeers bars.

Louie, I'm still working on finding a woman
who can understand me, cutting out carbohydrates,
reading comic books,
shuffling cards for you
alone after sunset,
plotting future calendars.

Seer of Angels and Demons

My Great-Grandmother
spoke of top hat men floating
and disappearing through the fog and pines,
earthbound fires lent by the sky
waltzing through the barns in an age
when Death strolled rural Wisconsin
like a wounded suitor.

My Father dreams of dogs he had to have put asleep,
chastises lingering deceased former homeowners
for creeping up on him while remodeling basements.
He saw a denim-jacketed lantern-eyed demon
drinking solo in a roadside northern Illinois bar,
set fire to a Ouija board that got weird on him,
screams from a bodiless shadow
still ring in his ears.

My Mother feels lives fleeting
before the phone's verification
or obituary ink drying on newsprint.
Maybe this explains her in Wal-Mart after midnight,
writing letters until sunrise.

Grandma heard children giggling in her living room
as she lay awake in bed. Grandpa was buried two days
earlier.
Normally fear would overtake her

but she fell back asleep untroubled.
My Grandpa, months before death,
patted the heads of children only he could see.

I have wasted rolls of film in cemeteries after dark,
confounded tarot readers with my white noise aura,
walked bored and empty through rooms
that gave psychics the creeps.
I stood drunk and defiant chanting a dead witch's name
while facing blackened mirrors.
When I opened my eyes, I saw my own reflection
confused, heartsick, hungry to touch the unholy or
divine,

the same bloody set of eyes I stare down each morning,
the only wraith following me through reflective glass.

TROY SCHOULTZ is a lifelong Wisconsin resident. He is currently a lecturer at the University of Wisconsin-Fox Valley, where he also edits the nationally recognized Fox Cry Review. His interests and influences include garage rock, vinyl LPs, found objects, the paranormal, abandoned places, folklore, old cemeteries and the number five. His poems, stories, and reviews have all appeared in Seattle Review, Nerve Cowboy, Rattle, Slipstream, Chiron Review, Word Riot, Fish Drum, Midwestern Gothic and several others since 1997. He was nominated in 2012 for a Pushcart Prize by Slipstream literary magazine, and is the author of two chapbooks, A Field of Bonfires Sings (Wolf Angel Press, 1999) and Good Friday (Tamafyhr Mountain Poetry, 2005). He currently resides in Oshkosh, WI.

www.ingramcontent.com/pod-product-compliance
Lightning Source LLC
Chambersburg PA
CBHW031209020426
42333CB00013B/861